# Psychic Like Me

by

**Tiffany Wardle**

# Psychic Like Me

## Contents

# Chapter 1
# Welcome

Hi and welcome to my 6 week home study course "Psychic Like Me"

I am overwhelmed to have you join me on this journey of psychic development. The first thing to learn is to take your time! Week 1 may take you a month to complete – there is no hurry! It's best to get it right, yes?

During this course you will learn to meditate and be given information to enhance your ability to meet your guides. You will also discover the way to use tools such as crystals, angel cards, the crystal ball and how to read from jewellery. The ability to see, hear, feel and 'know' on a psychic level is a wonderful gift, I will show you how.

I will teach you how to open up your Chakras, the seven energy points of the body and you will also receive a channeled message from one of my guides Angel Celeste about psychic development.

You will learn how to 'close down' and 'protect yourself' . This will ensure you are protected, re-grounded and re-focused after each psychic development session.

It is best if you wait 7 days before you start the next section to complete your homework, digest what you have learnt and practice, practice, practice!

I will not hold back on knowledge and tips for your development during the course, I want to make you an incredible psychic and exceed expectations,both yours and mine!

Enjoy!

# Chapter 2

# Getting To Know Your Teacher

So firstly a little about me.

I have been psychic my whole life – 35 years to be exact. I voiced my first premonition when I was a toddler and at the age of 16 started to use tarot cards every single day, I still use the same pack. I always knew there was something more to life and I felt the need to explore this feeling.

I could always sense guides, angels and spirits around me, sometimes I did not know who I was talking to but I knew there was someone there. I have since fine tuned my skills. Even though I knew I was psychic I tried to maintain a 'normal life'. I completed my 'A' Levels and then decided to go to University.

After studying Law at University I worked for National Newspapers in advertising but I knew a 'normal job' was not for me.

During my time in the national press I started to realise I was going through a huge transition; I could hardly sleep and I was hearing spirits every night. It soon became clear that I was channeling messages in my sleep. I was also reading for friends on a daily basis and the spiritual world appealed to me more and more. At this point in my life I felt so lost and had no idea which path to take. My hands would burn all through the night and I didn't know why. The pain was so excruciating I attended hospital for tests to see if this was an allergy or a reaction to something but the tests didn't reveal a cause and the doctors did not know what to do with me. It was my mother who suggested that I should look up natural healing. The moment I learnt Reiki the pain in my hands stopped. The heat I was feeling was energy trying to flow through me.

I completed my Reiki Masters and learnt about chi – the energy flow and the Chakras. How there are 7 main energy point of the body and how each one can effect us in different ways.
I then travelled to Japan on my quest for knowledge and I climbed the mountain where Reiki was discovered by Dr. Usui. I meditated up the mountain for 3 days – this changed my psychic ability forever – for the better. I have never been the same since.

For over 10 years I have been developing my gift; going to The Chelsea College of Psychic

Studies, training in Thailand, working in California as a psychic, setting up a psychic and healing clinic in Knightsbridge, Central London whilst also working on Psychic TV. I have read for many celebrities and devoured numerous teacher training courses within the spiritual realm. By looking into teacher training, I soon realised that I had insight that also needed to be shared, that I should be creating training courses. This is now where you come in.

I would like to teach you about my gift – I will not hold back! I would love you to become a better psychic than me! Teaching you how to open and close the energy points on your body and the benefits of this.

I will be working very closely with my angels and my guides through this process. I have Angel Celeste with me now, she is adding her energy to mine to make this a very powerful course. As an added bonus, Celeste is also giving us information about the Universe as it is now and how we psychics can help!

With the world changing so much throughout December 2012, a new spiritual dawn is upon us.
The Mayan Calendar is a 26,000 year calendar which ends 21st December 2012, meaning a

new age – a more spiritual age is upon us. What does this mean to you? This means, we need as many psychics, healers, light workers (those who aide others), chakra therapists, Reiki masters as possible to help everyone in to the new spiritual time. This includes you!

Join me now on my journey to enhance your psychic skills.
I hope you enjoy the healing energy invoked within this course from me and my angel. You may find you feel warmth, tingling or see visions whilst reading or practicing this course. This is the divine healing energy, be open to accepting its good.

# Chapter 3
## Tips

---

• You may want to practice with tools during this course; I would suggest having angel cards, a clear quartz crystal and perhaps a crystal ball for week 6. YOU DO NOT HAVE TO HAVE ANY OF THESE IF YOU DO NOT WANT THEM.

• I would stress that to stay grounded and focused please watch you sugar and caffeine intake during this course.

• Each section of this course should be practiced over at least a week before moving on to the next section, although there is no time limit on this course.

• Some sections may take you longer than others to go through.

• Some sections may resonate with you more than others – you may not want to become a crystal ball reader for example but it is still good to learn about all tools.

I must stress that all of us psychics are different. You may prefer working with the cards to working with your guides, each section will be challenging in different ways for you.

This course shows you all the different ways you can enhance your psychic ability. You may not be able to do all of it straight away so take your time!

This is not a race!

• These are life skills so keep going over each section – I know I had to!

• LEAVE YOUR EGO AT THE DOOR – it doesn't matter if you can't do it at first – let it flow in your own time – We ALL have psychic ability – let yourself go at your own pace.

• You must, must close down after each practice – notes on this are listed in week 3's meditation.

# Chapter 4
# The Course

# Section 1

# Meditation

### The Importance Of Meditation

I cannot stress enough the importance of meditation. Each week you will need to start with a meditation. Meditation helps to still the mind, this will calm you so that you can feel your inner guidance. During your psychic development you will be predicting people's futures. To make predictions you will be utilising the right hemisphere of the brain, this will help you to read people's energy. The right side of the brain is the creative side, by meditating we are concentrating more on calming down the mind, using less of the 'practical' left hemisphere of the brain and start to use your psychic ability.

### The History Of Meditation

Meditation has been used for centuries. Speculative research suggests that primitive hunting societies may have discovered meditation while staring at the flames of their fires. By focusing on the flames and calming their minds, a higher state of consciousness was perhaps achieved.

Over thousands of years, meditation evolved into a structured practice. By meditating, you are encouraging the right side of the brain to help you become more still and calm and thus listening to your inner self.

## How To Still Your Mind

Meditation should become part of your everyday life. Even if at first you manage 5 minutes every day; then aim to increase this to perhaps 1 hour every day, listening to your inner thoughts and your soul / higher self for guidance on what steps to take. This can help with feelings of happiness, inner peace and an inner knowing to trust oneself for guidance.

Living in the moment will help you live your life in a more peaceful way. The mind can have approximately 60,000 – 80,000 thoughts a day! This means our minds are all over the place. I want you try to live in the here and now.

Try This Now.

Take a deep breath in. Be aware of your surroundings. Stay with the moment. Try and hear noise from outside? Or from within the house and as you do be aware of your surroundings and the background noises around you but don't let your mind wander.

Stay with the moment.

Stop the noise in your mind. Every time your mind starts telling you the things you need to do today or the things that are 'bugging' you – bring it back to the moment. Do this for 5 minutes – it is quite difficult! A tip is to concentrate on your breathing. Hear your breath! Count as you breathe in and out. Another tip is to have your eyes slightly open and to look at the tip of your nose as this helps with concentration.

Please mentally prepare yourself for meditation now.

## MEDITATION PREPARATION

For this section you may want to light candles, soften lighting and ensure you are not going to be disturbed. Tell yourself right

now that you are going to meditate –
remember there is no time limit on this –
take as much time as you need and READ
SLOWLY TAKING PAUSES AND DEEP BREATHS
BETWEEN SECTIONS.

*You may want to read through the
meditation a few times before you complete
it.


## MEDITATION

Please sit comfortably with both feet flat on
the floor, laying your hands in your lap with
your palms upwards. Taking 3 deep breaths,
in through your nose and out through your
mouth - each breath deeper than the last.

Imagine you are standing at the mouth of a
beautiful pink and purple cave. As you look
into the cave you can see sparkles of pink and
purple all around you. You somehow start to
feel calm and you want to enter the cave. As
you start to walk in you see a treasure chest
in front of you. It is a large intriguing gold
chest and you feel that it is inviting you to
open it. In the chest you place any worries or
daily chores that are in your mind, know that
you will be coming back to these later but

you do not need these now. Close the chest and make your way through the cave.

As you walk through the cave you realise that the walls of the cave are made of stunning crystals; you go to touch the wall to feel the crystals. They are pink and purple in colour. Examine the crystals now - what do they feel like? These are rose quartz and amethyst crystals. Feel the love and compassion coming from the crystalline walls of the cave and breathe it in now. Feel the loving, calming, peaceful energy as the crystal cave surrounds you; this cave is your path to your psychic development.

As you walk through the cave, you can see a yellow crystal door and you decide to go through it feeling safe, warm and full of love. On the other side of the door you sense there is loving being there. Look at this now - study this image, what does it look like? Is this a person? A symbol? An animal? A mythical creature? Greet them with love and thank them for being with you. This is your guide who will help you. Your guide has a gift for you, the gift of psychic development. This gift is for you to use safely and with love. Stand in front of your guide now and breathe in the gift of psychic ability. Focus on this gift with love, kindness and compassion.

Embrace your guide and go back into the cave knowing that you can return here at any time. Thank your guide for staying with you while you complete each section of this course.Head back to the entrance of the cave and feel the ground under your feet. Wiggle your toes and clench your fists. Take 3 short sharp breaths and come back into the room.

**Exercise:**

I would like you to come up with your own meditation.

Ideas for your own meditation:

•Take yourself to your 'happy place' (This could be on a beach, in a cave, by the sea, in a forest, in a log cabin, in a beautiful home).

•Leave your daily chores and worries at the beginning of the meditative journey.

•Go on a walk in your mind as this will help your concentration, feel, smell, hear and see as much of the surroundings as possible.

•During the journey meet your guide, this could be an angel, a mythical creature, a spirit guide. Be creative!

• See something upon your travels like a treasure chest, a note, a letter, a symbol.

• Take time to sit and breathe deeply while you decipher the message / symbol you have received.

• Thank your guide for being with you.

• Go back to the start of your journey.

• Start to bring yourself back in to the room.

• Make notes or write out your meditation and practice!

Now it is your turn!

Go ahead — make up your own meditation. Know that there are no right or wrong answers — this is all part of your development!

### Homework

During the next week I would like to live in the moment at least 5 times for 5 minutes each time, sound easy? It's not! This will help to still your thoughts so that we can utilise the right hemisphere of the brain to increase psychic ability.

I would like you to do your meditation at least 5 times this week. This may mean you may have to set your alarm 15 minutes earlier in the morning or go to bed 15 minutes earlier.

Enjoy being creative! See you next week!

*You may want to take longer than a week to complete this section. Think of week 1 as section 1 and go at your own pace.

# Section 2

# What type of Psychic are you?

_____

**What type of psychic are you?**

- Clairvoyant
- Clairsentient
- Clairaudient
- Claircognizant
- How to enhance these abilities

There are 4 main types of psychic ability - or 4 different 'clairs' as us psychics like to call it. You may find one 'clair' dominates the others: for example you may see things in your mind but you may not be able to hear things just yet. They all develop at different times. I was very much a 'clairsentient' or 'feeling' psychic first before I developed my clairvoyance (seeing). You may be different.

**Explaining Psychic Abilities:**

**Clairvoyance**

Clairvoyance is the ability to see or picture things in a psychic way.

This will mean that when you look inside your mind you may be able to see scenes that you can describe. This also means that you MAY be able to see spirits, guides, angels, colours and auras in your mind. You may have scenes of future and past events running through your mind.

Clairvoyance means 'clear-seeing'. The ability to see Spirit through your third eye. The third eye is based between your eye brows. Clairvoyants can see energy, spirits, and symbols and get visual premonitions. Let's now develop clairvoyance; I will also give you my tips to do this.

As a clairvoyant you may see things in your mind's eye and you may see with your physical eyes. Both are possible, but it's more common to see in the mind's eye. Whereas as a clairsentient (a feeling psychic) you might pick up on feelings and emotions, as a clairvoyant you would probably see images of what is going to happen in your mind's eye, see auras, see spirits and angels. When reading a situation, a clairvoyant may see a symbol or a movie-scene which is the situation itself or a metaphor for the situation.

You may receive an image of a symbol like a heart or a key – you will now need to decipher this message with how you 'feel'. Again there is no right answer here – this symbol to you may be different to what it means to someone else. To me – a heart means love and a key means new home or new beginnings – this may be different to you depending on how you 'feel' about each symbol.

**How to Develop your Clairvoyant Abilities:**

Even if you're not a natural clairvoyant, you can still develop your clairvoyance. Flexing my clairvoyant muscles was the first thing I did when I started developing.

To open your third eye (the centre of clairvoyant abilities) you may start seeing coloured lights around people or in your mind and you may see spirit or energy near people that you think are guides or angels.

**Exercise for Developing Clairvoyance**

Lie down and take 3 deep breaths in through your nose and out through your mouth concentrating all your energy on the area between your eye brows.

Place an amethyst or clear quartz crystal in between your eye brows if you want to but you do not have to.

Imagine a third eye, between your eyebrows.

Visualise the eyelid on your third eye opening up.

Now pretend to get a cloth and clean your third eye as if it were a window, clean off any smudges.

Lay down for 5 minutes doing this.

When you sit up hold the crystal out in front of your third eye about 10cm – 20 cm's away from your face (you do not have to do this if you do not have a crystal)

Imagine a white light from the back of the crystal going through the crystal and in to your third eye.

Hold this for 3 – 5 minutes with the intention of opening up.

All visualisation does is set an intention to do something. If you visualise this regularly, you're putting energy behind your intention to open up your third eye, the centre of your clairvoyant abilities.

Please make notes on anything you see in your mind's eye for personal reference.

## Clairsentience

Clairsentience is the ability to feel spiritual things.

This skill allows you to go into a person's feelings and feel how they feel. You will be able to feel words and feel pictures. This will enable you to pick up difficulties around you and your clients very quickly. This is a skill I use every day. I use this skill not only to feel my clients emotions but also to feel what is right for me. Sometimes you may sense what is going on around a person – this is your clairsentience kicking in – your 'feeling' clair. You may even connect with another person's emotions so strongly that you may want to cry, feel happy, get butterflies – if it is too much – just state the intention to tone it down.

Clairsentience is perhaps the most down-to-earth of all the intuitive gifts. Most people use clairsentience on a daily basis. This looks like your feelings sending you intuitive guidance. Just to give a common example: you may experience a feeling of discomfort and then intuitively feel impulsed to look behind you only to see someone staring at you.

## How Clairsentients Receive Intuitive Guidance:

Gut Feelings include feelings of excitement: an uplifting feeling in your stomach area could mean that you are on the right track. This 'feeling' appears for a reason; it could be to warn you against something or someone.

Psychic sensations: Clairsentience also speaks to you through sensations in your body - like tickling or butterflies. I get laughter and sadness sensations when I pick up on a client – you may get this too.

## How to Develop Your Clairsentience:

Here is a quick exercise you can do to

develop your clairsentience further:

1. Close your eyes and take 3 deep breaths in through your nose and out through your mouth.

2. Ask the universe to open up your clairsentience

3. Start to think about a loved one – friend, family member, partner or even colleague.

4. How do you feel now? Are you feeling happy, emotional, do you get a sense of nervousness around this person?

5. Ask yourself what this individual is like as a person

6. If you feel you want to – you can ask the person the next time you see them how they are feeling – how accurate were you?

Please make notes on anything you see in your mind's eye for personal reference.

## Clairaudience

Clairaudience is the ability to hear spiritual

things.

Clairaudience means 'clear-hearing'. It is the ability to 'hear' spirit.

Clairaudience is that little voice inside you that issues warnings or gives guidance. If you don't have clairaudience as one of your psychic gifts, it can be developed. Do not worry – we are all different!

Clairaudience is one of your natural intuitive gifts, your inner self and perhaps your guides will use mostly clairaudient means to communicate with you, including sounds, words and songs you're familiar with. These can be internal or they can be outside of you. You may also hear voices in your dreams or upon waking.

### Exercise

Lay down take 3 deep breaths. Listen carefully to all the sounds you hear around you.

The sounds of cars passing, the sounds of birds or animals, of a plane, of people talking, the sound of music.

Start to feel your senses really engage.

When you begin to listen consciously to the noise that you normally tune out, you will hear an 'orchestra' of sounds.

Your objective with this exercise is to notice each and every one of these sounds that make up this 'orchestra'.

Take it apart. Count how many sounds you can hear and make a note of what they are.

Some may be really subtle and barely noticeable. The goal here is to really to heighten your auditory perception.

Do this every day this week and you will be amazed at how much you were not hearing before. This will begin to activate your clairaudience.

## Another Clairaudient Exercise

Sit up and make a statement to yourself that you are tuning in to your psychic hearing.

Take 3 deep breaths in through your nose and out through your mouth. Close your eyes once you have read the instruction. Focus on your inner ear; you may hear high pitched noises when you concentrate.

Imagine a swirl of energy around your ears as if they are being fine tuned.

Visualise turning on a radio and tuning into the 'channel' of your inner voice and any guides who want to come forward at this time.

Imagine your inner guidance as a person sitting around a table with any guides you may have, ready to communicate with you. Then, start asking questions.

See if you can 'hear' or perceive any words — it could be a clear voice that is easy to discern or you may have to really focus and go inside yourself to hear it clearly. You may get the impression of a song. If you don't hear anything at all, don't give up on your first attempt. For most people it takes practice and persistence to get into the habit of listening to your intuition.

Please note! Not everyone is clairaudient — you may never hear anything everyone is different — there are no right or wrong answers.

**Tiff's Top Tips**

- Set the intention to utilise your clairaudience. Write it down somewhere as this reinforces it.

- Meditate. Intuitive guidance often comes through the gaps between our thoughts.

- Use an affirmation (a positive intention) to develop clairaudience, such as 'It is safe to hear my inner voice' or 'I am powerfully clairaudient'.


Please make notes on anything you see in your mind's eye for personal reference.


**Claircognizance**

**What is Claircognizance?**

Claircognizance means 'clear-knowing'. It is to just 'know' a situation. I get the feeling sometimes that I just 'know' something and I don't know why. This is my claircognizance kicking in.

Claircognizants 'know' certain things without being told. For claircognizants, your guides or your inner self may download information in your mind. It can be an inspired idea. Claircognizance is characterised by this strong sense of knowing that goes beyond logic and by the fact that the intuitive information comes into the thinking mind, not into the heart or the mind's eye.

**How to Develop your Claircognizance:**

• Sit with a pen and paper in front of you.

• Set the intention to develop your claircognizance to start the process!

• Write your intention down as this will make it more powerful.

• Ask your higher self a question and write down the answer.

• Write with confidence as if you already know the answer.

**Tiff's Top Tips**

• Often your claircognizance is already operating and waiting to be recognised as guidance. This is also known as automatic writing and can come in handy when you have a decision to make in your life.

**Homework**

1. Memorise all the 'clairs' and what they mean

2. Ask yourself a simple question and write down what you:

a. See(Clairvoyance)

b. Hear (Clairaudience)

c. Feel (Clairsentience)

d. Know (Claircognizance)


* Remember you may not see, feel, hear or know anything just yet! This is very early on in your development and this is not a race!

# Section 3

# Chakra Work

There are 7 main energy points on the body — called chakras. These energy points or chakras have a significant impact on the development of your psychic ability. Building and opening your chakras will increase psychic perceptions and premonitions. The following chakra information will help you determine if and where you have blocks in your chakras so that you can start the process of opening yourself back up to higher energies and allowing energy to flow through your body. This will help you connect with higher energies such as spirit, guides and angels. Exciting stuff!

## The 7 Main Chakras

### The Base Chakra

The Importance of the Base Chakra is to help ground you and calm you. When doing psychic work you must be grounded so that your mind is peaceful and can see the messages clearly. Also being grounded will help in other areas of your life – when your base chakra is fully functional it can help you to get organised. Sorting out the bills, getting your finances into order. Do you suffer from lower back pain? Do you worry about money? There is often a link here.

**Where:** This is at the base of your spine.

**Colour:** It is red.

**Crystal:** A good crystal to use on this part of your body would be a red jasper or ruby (This is information only - you do not have to have this crystal)

**Affirmation:** Now state "Thank you for opening my base chakra"

**Process: To Open This Chakra**

• I would suggest lying on your back and hover your hands over your pubis area at the very base of your spine. Imagine a red spiral circling round and round and getting bigger and faster in this area. The visualisation may take you a while. You may feel tingling, butterflies, heat, cold or just a sense that something is happening. This is your base chakra opening up.

• After 3 – 5 minutes state "I open myself up to love"

• Keep your hands here until you 'feel' it is time to move them. Sometimes I cannot physically move my hands away for 5 – 10 minutes. If you are unsure, 5 minutes is a good starting point. You may feel your hands heat up or tingle. This is the universal energy flowing through you. Do not be at all alarmed; remember this therapy cannot do you any harm whatsoever. Only universal energy is flowing through you which is positive and loving.

• You may feel blockages slowly moving in your stomach region. You may feel your feet tingling as any blockages start to leave your body. This is all good stuff!

### The Sacral Chakra

The sacral chakra: Good for desire, sexual energy, creativity and intention.

**Where:** This chakra is just below your navel.

**Colour:** It corresponds with the colour orange

**Crystal:** A carnelian crystal is good for this area but you do not need to buy this crystal if you do not want to.

**Affirmation:** "I open my psychic gift with love"

**Process: To Open This Chakra**

• Place your hands about an inch below your navel. This is the sacral chakra area.

• Hover your hands over the area for 5 minutes or so. You may feel tingling, heat, butterflies, a sense that something is happening, your tummy may start rumbling! You may feel blockages moving around inside. Again, nothing is bad! Your chakras are opening up and blockages may leave your body via your head, hands and feet so you may feel sensations around these areas.

• Visualise an orange spiral or Katharine wheel in the sacral chakra area and let it get bigger and faster in your mind's eye. This is again, opening up your chakra.

**Tiff's Top Tip:**

I can now open up this chakra just by visualising orange around the lower navel area; you too will get to this stage. If you have tummy / digestion problems this could all be linked to your sacral chakra. The soul yearns for creative projects, why not meditate whilst thinking about this area on your body to find out what it is your soul desires? Music / art / painting / writing / decorating / cooking? Let us see what new hobbies are in store!

### The Solar Plexus

This is the seat of your intuition. This chakra is SO important for your psychic work. If you switched off your thinking for a while and just concentrated on your intuition your psychic ability will improve tenfold! Also your OWN life could be SO MUCH BETTER!

Now you see the importance of this topic? You hold the answers to your questions. How? As the answers are within you! We just need to find them! How? By opening your solar plexus chakra!

So many of us seek answers elsewhere when they really they lie within us, in our solar plexus. So, a very important chakra cleanse is needed here indeed!

**Where:** The solar plexus is located just above your navel.

**Colour:** Yellow.

**Crystal:** A good crystal for this area would be a citrine.

**Affirmation:** Thank you for my courage

**Process: To Open This Chakra**

• Make the statement of intention that you WILL now open up your solar plexus.

• Place your hands 1 inch above your navel. My solar plexus is going crazy right now as I write this!

• Imagine the yellow spiral / Katharine wheel and let it get bigger and bigger and faster! I would suggest 10 – 12 minutes on this chakra or until your hands feel it is time to move on.

**Tiff's Top Tips**

So Why Is Your Solar Plexus So Important? It is where you keep the answers from your higher self. Have you ever asked your higher self a direct question.

As you sit reading this course think of a question you want answered.

Let's try this process now. I will do it with you. My question is "Will I travel back to work in California?"

Now I am going to sit up straight with this question in my head. I am now focussing all of my attention on the area just above my navel. I am thinking about the colour yellow in a spiral as I open my solar plexus. It is slow at first. After 2 minutes I feel I have an answer!

YES!

Now you try it!

It may take you 10 – 12 minutes. It may take you a few goes. You really must trust your feelings here! You may think you are making it up or you are feeling nothing. This is just your ego or your lower self kicking in to say hello, ignore it! Go with your GUT instinct! Make sure the answer isn't coming from your head or your heart and you have your answer. Try something small at first that can be validated before you get on to the big life changing questions!

Do you ever get that feeling that you have met someone before but you haven't? Do you ever feel that familiarity with new people and you don't know why? A lot of the time, this is your solar plexus saying hello moments before you meet someone. Imagine your solar plexus shaking hands with the person you are about to meet a few moment before you even see them...this is what it does! It's one step ahead and therefore can know what's just ahead of you.

The solar plexus is great for all of this. I don't know where I would be without mine; today my solar plexus even told me what food to eat!

Your clients may ask you a direct question – e.g. Will I marry? Is my money situation going to improve? Concentrate on your solar plexus to check the guidance you are being given so that it 'feels' right.


**Closing Down**

Closing down the solar plexus chakra is very important. If you leave your chakras wide open, people are able to 'zap your energy'.

To close this down, simply: pretend there is a light switch next to your solar plexus and switch off the light. Put a black cloak over the yellow spiral. Then put a large shield over your whole stomach area and then lock it up.

## Grounding

It is very important to ground yourself after your chakras have been wide open. Pretending that there are weights on the bottom of your feet as you walk is a good way to ground yourself. I put both my feet on the floor and imagine tree roots coming out of the bottom of my feet to re root me to the earth.

We will go over closing down and grounding at the end of the chakra section of this course.

## The Heart Chakra

**Where:** Heart centre / centre of your chest.

**Colour:** Pink and green.

**Crystal:** A rose quartz crystal is good for this chakra; this is good for love (you do not need to buy this crystal to complete the following exercise).

**Affirmation:** I am open to all aspects of love

Your psychic work will greatly benefit from opening the heart chakra. Why is this? This will help you to lovingly speak when giving a psychic reading — this will uplift people, leaving them in a positive state with a smile on their face.

### Process: To Open This Chakra

My beautiful angel Celeste has come to join me as I write. She is excited about this part of the course as she would like to channel some information through me.

*Channeled From Angel Celeste:*

*The heart chakra is what us angels love and adore you humans to feel. Love is the highest frequency and therefore the love you feel is necessary to strengthen your connection to your angels. Everyone has a guardian angel and then different angels come and go when you ask them to. There are unemployed angels waiting to be called upon to help you through your life. There are education angels waiting to help you learn more skills. There are creative angels waiting to help with your soul's desire to fulfill creative projects.*

*There are the Archangels who are here for healing (Archangel Raphael), wisdom (Archangel Uriel), love (Archangel Chamuel), protection (Archangel Michael).*

*I am here to ensure your heart chakra becomes as open and as fulfilled as it was meant to be.*

*The more you strengthen your connection with angels the more the angels can assist you with your psychic work. We do hear you, we know your requests. Humans have been given free will so angels are not allowed to intervene unless asked. If you have a challenge or a problem at the moment just ask the angels, they will be more than happy to assist you.*

*Process: To Open This Chakra*

*To open your heart chakra I would like you to fill yourself up with love. Think of the people in your life that you love the most — offer them love in your own way now. Think of them; hold the thought in your mind's eye right now. As you think of them how are you*

44

*feeling? It is the feelings and not necessarily the words that the universe hears so let the feelings of love pour out of you. Now offer some of the love you are feeling to the whole world.*

*OK as you hold this feeling of love lay down and programme yourself to love. Place your hands on your heart chakra at the centre of your chest. Imagine a pink and green spiral whizzing around, as this gets larger feel the love flowing through your body. Feel it open up. You may feel the energy, the heat or the tingling. If this doesn't happen don't worry! There are no right and wrong answers to this, you may one day feel there is something.*

*Do this for 5 – 10 minutes. Every time you feel a little frustrated with someone, you can very quickly do this exercise and offer them love. We are all attached to the universal energy, so being negative toward others just means we are being negative toward ourselves.*

*Message ends.*

The exercise that Angel Celeste just channeled through me was to help you open your heart chakra so that you can give loving readings if you so wish. This will also help you in your everyday life. You can do this as many times as you wish.

## Throat Chakra

**Throat:** Communication

**Colour:** Blue

**Crystal:** Aquamarine

**Affirmation:** I speak with words of love and kindness.

Firstly you will need to open your throat chakra so that you can lovingly speak the truth during your psychic work.With your psychic work you may start to sense your client has a blockage around the throat area, meaning there something your client needs to get off their chest (if you are going to have clients). You may feel your throat tighten; you may see the colour blue. You may sense there is a truth your client needs to hear themselves?

Your client may have a partner and they may want to communicate more openly? You may not feel anything at first – but have the intention that you know this will open up.

This is all to do with the Throat Chakra.

•**Alternative Affirmation:** My ability to communicate flows freely within me.

**Process: How To Open Your Throat Chakra**

• Put your hands above your throat chakra, in the middle of your neck.

• Imagine the blue circle swirling.

• Feel the chakra opening: you may feel heat, tingling, pins and needles, you may feel nothing, either way keep trying. Do this for 5 or so minutes.

## Third Eye Chakra

**Third Eye:** This is in the middle of your 2 eyes. This will help you to be clairvoyant, this helps to see inside your mind, this helps with predictions and intuition.

**Where:** Middle of your forehead

**Colour:** Indigo

**Crystal:** Iolite

**Affirmation:** I see clearly with loving eyes

The third eye chakra is good for spirituality, psychic ability, intuition.

The third eye is so important for your psychic development. We will be working a lot with the third eye during this course so take a break now if you wish and come back fully charged!

**Tiff's Top Tip**

You must trust what you see! First rule! Just have the confidence to trust in your third eye and you are half way there!

It is so important to open this is up to connect your intuition and clairvoyance (seeing). If you struggle with this just ask the angels and they will help you, even if you don't feel them!

Angels cannot help without your permission; they are always whispering words of love to you, giving you the feelings of warmth and sending you images of peace. By connecting with your third eye angels are able to communicate with you.

My angel, Angel Celeste, would like to try this with you now.

Meditation channeled from Angel Celeste

*Programme a purple crystal such as an Iolite or Amethyst to "seeing with love" if you wish. OR make the affirmation "I see with love".*

*Where: Either place a crystal on your third eye, your brow chakra, in the middle of your forehead. Or hover your hands above your third eye – this will work just the same.*

*Process: Imagine an indigo light spiraling around your third eye and focus on it while I, Celeste, the angel say to you:*

*"See a purple fire in front of you – concentrate on the flame, through the flame you see an opening, it looks like a beautiful place, it is all white, a white open space that feels warm and welcoming, walk into the purple flame to the place of light.There you can see Archangel Michael who wants to introduce you to your angel.*

*You look down at yourself in your mind's eye and you are wearing beautiful white robes, you look at your hands through your mind's eye and your hands have a white / silver glow all around them, you sense that this white glow is around your whole being. You look up to see the sky is white, pure, spiritual, you see*

49

*white doves in the sky flying with love. You remain looking up as you feel so much love coming down on you from the universe.*

*As you look down a new angel has appeared next to Archangel Michael. Your angel is smiling at you, wearing the same white robes as you, with a white glow all around them, just like you! This is your angel! Assigned to you, to lovingly help you, guide and be there for you when you are feeling down or need loving guidance.*

*What does your angel look like? Look hard in your mind's eye. Archangel Michael is helping you open your mind's eye right now to see your angel. Maybe you can sense your angel? Hear your angel? Or see them? There are no wrong answers here! What colour hair do they have? What do they look like?*

*Stay with your angel for as long as you like. See if you can strengthen your connection by asking them a question? You may feel or sense the answer, you may not, this will strengthen over time. Bask in the light of your angel for as long as you like. Thank Archangel Michael for bringing them to you. Thank your angel for showing themselves to you.*

*When you are ready, take 3 short sharp breaths and open your eyes.*

*Well done – you just opened your third eye chakra! Keep trying this until you see your angel.*

*Message ends.*

Use this meditation every time you want to encourage your third eye to open and of course strengthen your connection with your angel!

This may take a few sessions to work so keep at it! Your angels may change over time, just trust in what you see!

I, Tiffany, did the meditation that Angel Celeste gave me and I was introduced to a new Angel who has come in for a short while to give me strength – I asked his name – he said Andrew.

Who is yours? What did you ask?

Now we need to look at the Crown Chakra.

# Crown Chakra

**Colour:** Violet

**Crystal:** Amethyst

**Where:** Top of the head

**Affirmation:** I see and feel my guides easily and clearly.

The Crown Chakra relates to spirituality, selflessness, empathy. It is the area where you connect with your higher self, your loving self, your soul. This is where spirituality enters the body, relating to intelligence and deep thought. It is associated with the pineal gland and with all of the master glands. This is to enhance your connection with your higher self and also the higher frequencies such as spirit guides. This will help you connect psychically to your client and your client's guides, angels and spirits (if you choose to have clients).

## Process: To Open This Chakra

• Programme your crystal or yourself to spirituality.

• Focus on the Violet swirling energy above your head.

- Feel spirituality pour into you from the top of your head. You may feel light headed. Feel the positivity, the love as you open yourself up to the universal energy.

- Feel motivated! Feel energised!

- Feel a loving connection to the Universe! Do this for 5 minutes.

## Closing Down

This is a very important process and must be done after each opening session. Leaving your chakras open can leave you feeling ungrounded and unfocused.

## Closing Down Exercise

- Imagine a light switch next to each chakra and turn it off!

- Start at the base chakra at the base of your spine, focus your energy here and switch of an imaginary light switch at your base chakra.

- Then go to your sacral chakra below your navel. "Turn off the light".

• Focus your energy on your solar plexus above your navel and place a shield over it after turning the light switch off, to ensure this is closed down.

• Imagine putting a black cloak over your heart chakra and turn the imaginary light switch off here.

• Switch off the light at your blue throat chakra and feel the energy spiral slowing down.

• Cover your third eye chakra in the middle of your forehead with a black cloak and turn the switch off.

• Imagine a light switch over your head to turn off your crown chakra.

• Thank all your angels and guides for being with you during this chakra opening session.

• Imagine a green shower of light washing over your now.

• Wrap yourself in a beautiful silk white sheet of light and imagine your feet are rooted to the ground.

• Give thanks.

- Hold the intention that you are now closed down.

- Feel your feet rooted to the ground .

## Tiff's Top Tips

- Grounding is so important during psychic work. If you every feel a little ungrounded or 'all over the place' imagine bricks on the bottom of your feet re rooting you to the earth.

- When I am in close proximity to others I quite often feel people's energy and therefore I ask for protection from my guides and wrap myself in an imaginary silk white sheet – try this!

## Homework

1. Learn all the chakra names at your own pace – this is not a race!

2. Spend the rest of the day pretending you have bricks on the bottom of your feet to re ground you.

# Section 4
# Working With Your Third Eye

### How To Open Third Eye With Chanting

So we have already opened the third eye so now let's use it to do psychic readings!

One technique that helps utilise the third eye is called 'Aum' mantra meditation. This method uses the seed sound to open the third eye. The Third Eye chakra's seed sound is "AUM". By chanting this sound, you will directly stimulate your third eye, causing it to activate and open.

### Exercise

1. Sit up straight.

2. Now close your eyes.

3. Hold the intention to open up your psychic eye (third eye).

4. Chant out loud the mantra "AUM". (Long sound of "OOOOOOOOOO" and end with a shorter sound "MMMM").

5. While you are chanting this mantra, you will want to keep your attention focused on the third eye which is located at the centre of your forehead.

6. Ask for a message to be placed in your third eye .

7. Say the chant again8.Be still until you receive an image.

9. Be thankful for the message.


**Tiff's Top Tips**

Sometimes I sit with an Amethyst Crystal on my forehead where my third eye is and focus all my energy on this area. I ask my guides and angels to join me in my mind's eye. We often sit together happily in a forest and there is a message for me. The reason this works is because I am in my 'happy' place. Try it!


**Homework**

This week is more about practice than writing – so keep practicing!

## A Homework Exercise for you

• Hold the intention to open your third eye even more than before.

• Hold the intention to purely use psychic ability with the third eye.

• Switch off your 'feeling' ability, switch off your hearing and knowing, switch off all the 'clairs' except your clairvoyance.

• Ask any guides you may feel around you to help you to open your third eye so that you can see psychic predictions. If you do not feel a guide around you just ask the universe!

• Do this all week until you are comfortable with what you are seeing.

• If you are seeing symbols try and decipher the symbols. If you are seeing colour – try and see what these colours mean to you.

• There are no right or wrong answers! This is your development!

Make sure you make notes on your third eye images and experiences for reference at a later date.

# Section 5
# Connecting With Your Guides

---

You may want to enhance your connection with your angels and spirit guides so that they can give you the information you need during your psychic development. Maybe you already know who your guides are? Your guides may change during the course of your life. There are many 'unemployed' angels who need things to do. May be you want to employ an angel to help with your psychic development? You can ask new guides to come in right now to purely focus on this area of your life.

We are going to start this section with a meditation to bring in any guides to help with your psychic work or to strengthen your connection with your current angels and guides.

**Tiff's Top Tips**

I have a Native American Chief as a guide, I have my Grandfather, I have Angel Celeste from Atlantis, I have Archangel Raphael, I sometimes have Archangel Michael, I have my new guide Andrew and I have a new wizard too! So you can see that I have many guides that I use for different areas of my life – for example Archangel Raphael is always near me when I am doing my healing work. So don't think you only have one guide — some of you will have one, some will have many! Some would rather just use clairvoyance, there is not right or wrong. Guides may take years to come forward — so there is no hurry.

## Another Top Tip

Before the meditation I would like you to listen to at least one song that you love. Play the song out loud. Move your body a little or a lot if you feel like it. Dance around if you feel like it. Sing a long if you want to. Ensure this is a song that will invoke happy thoughts!

I want you to connect with some very high frequency beings. Angels and guides are on a higher frequency than us — imagine that by listening to the music you are tuning in like a radio to their frequency. If you are feeling low it is much harder to connect with high frequency beings. Laughter is also a good way to connect, love is the ultimate connection.

## Exercise

• Close your eyes once you have read the instruction
• With your eyes closed focus all of your energy on your body
• Focus the energy on your feet
• Then your legs

- Up your spine
- Focus and feel the energy around your heart chakra
- Then up to your neck and throat
- Focus on your third eye chakra and hold the intention to open your third eye chakra now
- Then breathe in very deeply
- See the indigo spiral in your third eye before moving the energy to the top of your head – the crown chakra. See a violet Orchid above your head, keep focussing on this. Imagine that this orchid is the key to your soul – your higher self.
- Imagine that your guardian angel / guide and your soul are best friends
- See your guardian angel or your guide now looking at the orchid, standing next to you. Imagine them staring intently with love at this orchid
- They reach out to touch the orchid – this is your guardian angel reaching out to love you. They connect with your soul – let them now connect with you and your soul. As they touch the orchid imagine that you and your soul are one. Feel that connection. As you become in 'sync' with your soul feel the touch of your angel then feel the three of you merging into one: Soul, Angel and you
- Take the deepest breath you can in 3 times to see and feel 3 beings becoming one
- This is an amazing experience

• You are becoming truly entwined with your soul – what does your soul feel like to you? Your inner self, your higher self? An ego-less self, just full of love. What is your inner self saying to you right now?

• As you become connected with your guide or your angel thank them for finally making contact. Everyone has a guardian angel but maybe you are seeing your guide, a spirit guide or another angel. Whoever you are seeing wants to connect with you to help and support you with your psychic development.

• Embrace your guide / angel

• Stay there basking in the love of your guide / angel for 2 – 3 minutes

• See a pure white light surrounding you, your soul, and your angel

• Take a deep breath in and on the exhale see a gold light coming out of your mouth and surrounding you and you angel

• Look at your angel now – what do they look like – see them with your clairvoyance. Feel what they are like as a being with your clear feeling. Ask them their name with your clairaudience. Know they have a message for you with your new found claircognizance

• Wait and bask in their presence until you have received your message

• Thank your angel for being with you during your psychic development

- Lovingly ask them to be with you during your own psychic readings – giving you information to enhance your psychic ability
- Feel them lovingly accept
- Take another look at them – even more closely this time, look at their eyes, clothes, hair – really fine tune your sight
- Offer them a gift as a thank you for being with you during this meditation – a gift of love, some flowers, an offering of peace to the universe, whatever feels right for you
- Step back from your angel and smile until you feel them fade away

Who is yours? What did you ask?

### Homework

To strengthen this connection you may want to ask them to come forward to you every day for approximately 5 minutes or as many times as you can. The feeling you get from your guide / angel will overwhelm you with love as they are loving beings so this will be a fantastic piece of homework for you! You may have seen a spirit or a guide as opposed to an angel – whomever you saw has come forward to help you with your psychic ability so ask them to be with you during your readings / psychic development.

**Please read before next week:**

Week 6 is all about utilising tools during psychic readings. You may want to have some psychic tools to use during this course to practice on.
Next week this course will explain how to use:
Angel Cards
Crystals
Crystal ball
Psychometry (jewellery)

You may want to have some of these tools to hand next week to complete this section of the course.

Please note you do not have to have any of these tools to complete this course if you do not want to buy them, as your psychic ability will increase with or without tools. You may find you want to be a 'hands free' psychic and not use any tools. This course is about YOU – making you feel comfortable.

Some people work with crystals, some with cards – become the psychic YOU want to be.

# Section 6
# Discover Your Tools

---

Some psychics like to use tools to help them with their readings. Some psychics always use tarot cards to read. Others use angel cards, runes, ribbons, feathers, crystal balls, jewellery, crystals. During this section I want you to explore what kind of psychic YOU are. You may prefer to work 'hands free' (without tools). You may prefer to work just with your guide – Let's find out!

*If you do not have cards please read this section for reference only – it is up to YOU what psychic you want to be.

### Angel / Oracle Cards

Many people feel the need to work closely with their angels and guides after a mystical experience introduces them to the 'idea' of their unseen teachers and protectors. Our guides and angels can appear in dramatic ways and many visit in dreams and visions.

Most angel card decks contain a series of single, positive messages or simple, optimistic phrases. Interpreting them is mainly a matter of practice. My first advice with using any sort of divination pack (angel cards) would be 'pack away the instruction book!' Real clairvoyants and psychics work from instinct.

**Preparing to use Angel Cards**
Please cleanse your angel cards before you start. You can do this by getting to know them. Feeling what each card means to you. Close your eyes and touch each and every card to imprint your energy on them. It really doesn't matter what the cards say – it is what the card means to YOU – No answer is wrong – your intuition will answer for you!

**Safekeeping**
It's important to keep your angel cards in a special place. You can wrap your cards in a piece of silk or black velvet if you wish.

**Working with Spreads**
What's a spread? Usually, cards are laid out in spreads (in patterns on the table). Although you will find lots of different 'patterns' in books, there is no right or wrong way to do this and you can easily make up your own.

**How to read the Angel Cards**
Always follow your instincts first. Maybe you are drawn to one area on the card and not the whole card. Maybe you are drawn to one

word on the angel card and not the whole sentence.

Remember there is no wrong answer. Your instincts always know best. Meditate on each card if you are not given an answer straight away. Close your eyes and say how you feel.

**Getting it right**
One final word? Practice, Practice, and more Practice!

### Exercise
Ask a question out loud and shuffle the cards. Pick out 1 card face down. Do not look at the card straight away! Close your eyes and feel the answer. Feel this from your stomach area – your solar plexus. What are you instinctively feeling about this card? Write this down and still do not look at the card.

Have a look in your third eye now and ask what the card means. Write down what you see in your third eye.

Focus your thoughts in your mind – what is your claircognizance (knowing) telling you about this card? Write this down.

Focus all of your energy on your hearing and be still for 60 seconds. Ask the universe for a clear message about this card. Write down anything you hear, a word, a song, a sentence, a voice.

Finally ask your guide / angel to come forward. If and when you feel someone around you ask them what this card means. Make a note of how you received your answer – (seeing, feeling, hearing, knowing?)

Then look at the card. What part of the card resonates with the answer? Is this the colour of the card? The picture or maybe the words? One area of the card? This answer will be different for everyone.

For example you may have just felt an overwhelming feeling of love and the card may be to do with work so you think you can't be right. Well of course you are right as you must MUST trust in what you are seeing, hearing, feeling and knowing! You must trust in spirit! The card may be saying to only invoke loving thoughts about your job situation for example. When you feel you have got the answer right try this exercise again.

Please note you may have only seen with your third eye, you may not have heard anything. Quite often you will have one dominant clair and the rest may follow suite, some clairs may not develop within you we are ALL different! Become the psychic you feel comfortable with – you do not have to be everything to everyone! If you do not hear – it does not matter you may 'feel' and 'see' which trust me is more than enough!!

## Crystal Ball

**Please note:** You do not have to have a crystal ball for this section. If you are drawn to becoming a crystal ball reader then please use one during this section. If you do not want to get a crystal ball then please just read this section and move on.

## Exercise

Choose your crystal ball that you intend to use; be sure to cleanse it first. (Hold with intent and ask it to be cleansed of previous energy OR leave it in moon light).

• In a darkened room, sit quietly with the crystal ball in front of you. Allow for a low light source, so that the crystal is somewhat 'back lit" yet the rest of the room should remain dark. A candle works well be sure to follow safety rules when working with an open burning flame. The colour of the candle should be something that reflects Higher Purpose like Purple for Higher self, White for God/Goddess and Soul purity or orange for attraction (but be sure you say aloud that you wish to only attract positive energies or you could get any energy just floating by).

• Ask a question and focus on the crystal ball. This may give you images in your third eye. This may help you to focus the mind more. Try it now.

• When you feel you have seen enough, or the crystal's images fade out, allow your mind to return to the present (physical plane).
• Feel your vibratory rate change once again as the crystal separates from one to two separate beings again.
• Refocus your eyes; blink as you need and breathe deeply, as you ground yourself once more.
• Finally clear and energise your mind.
• In Grounding yourself, a drink of water can help, as you pull the earth's energies up into your body once more.
• Remember it takes practice so don't be upset if it doesn't work right away. Take your time, allow the crystal and your energies to match, it will work.

**Tiff's Top Tip**
I find it is best to ask the question and then hold your gaze on one spot on the ball until you see an image in your mind – try this.

If you felt yourself start to tingle or vibrate, you may feel heat, cold or just detached from yourself. This is the crystal raising or lowering your vibratory level so that you may both be one in harmony and make the needed psychic connection.

## Crystals

The potent powers embedded within crystals are perfectly suited to the development of psychic ability.

There are many different types of crystals, but some are more useful than others when it comes to enhancing your own psychic powers. So which crystals are the best to use if you want to increase your psychic abilities? Below are some of the crystals you can use to activate and encourage your psychic ability.

You do not have to buy any crystals for this course – you can use this section for reference only if you so wish.

**Amethyst:** This beautiful purple crystal can help any beginner who wants to open up their psychic powers as it activates psychic ability, enhances intuition and opens up our spiritual awareness.

**Clear quartz:** This is fantastic for your psychic development! This crystal is known for its powerful healing properties, and its ability to amplify thoughts and energy. For this reason, it can help you to enhance both your psychic and healing abilities.

**Fluorite:** Can also open up psychic abilities rapidly!

**Obsidian:** This powerful black crystal is strongly protective and able to provide a shield to deflect negativity. It helps you to open your mind to new possibilities and encourages the development of strength and compassion – both important qualities that any good psychic needs to possess.

**Tigers Eye:** This crystal is useful when you begin to open up your psychic abilities because it can be used for grounding and protection; both of which are a very important part of the development of psychic powers. Some people like to sleep with a Tigers Eye crystal under their pillow for protection.

### Exercise

How to use crystals for psychic development: Make sure that your crystals are cleansed before using them for a new purpose. Clean your crystals by holding them under cold, running water before use, or leave in moonlight, or hold in your hand with the intention of cleansing.

1. Hold one of the crystals known for their psychic properties to the point between your eyes whilst meditating. This is the location of the "third-eye" chakra and a personal gateway to your own psychic

ability. Amethyst is particularly useful for this purpose.

2. Place a crystal into a glass of water and leave overnight or for as long as you can (check the crystal has not been polished or changed in any way before doing this). In the morning, remove the crystal from the glass. Hover you hand above the glass – state that this water will enhance your psychic ability. Drink the water which will, by now, be powerfully charged with the crystal's psychic energy. I must stress this is very powerful and is something you can do for other areas of your life as well as psychic advancement.

Keep crystals around your home, on your persons or in your bag. Crystals with psychic properties can be kept near to or under your pillow, to help enhance your ability. Hold a crystal in your hand before bed. Thank the crystal for helping to increase your psychic power and put under your pillow. Leave it there for as long as you feel the need to.

**Tiff's Top Tips**

1. I never use crystals without charging them first. I will always hold a crystal in my hand with the intention to enhance my connection with my client before use – I find this a great way to connect when doing a psychic reading – try it!

2. Crystals have a funny way of losing themselves when you no longer need them. If you find that a crystal goes missing do not panic – you just don't need that energy any more as it is time to move on!

3. Keeping crystals near your heart chakra I find most powerful – kept around your neck or in your bra (!) is a good idea.

## Psychometry

Psychometry: Psychic readings using objects such as jewellery.

### Exercise

This exercise involves getting hold of an object that someone has worn regularly, like jewellery or a watch. All objects absorb energy from their owners and if you are clairsentient (clear feeling), you can tune into this energy residue. Hold the object in your hand for a minute or two. If the item is holding a lot of strong positive or negative energy, you will probably pick up on that. You may also be able to feel what type of energy. Write down three things you see, feel, hear or know when holding an object belonging to someone else.

Psychometry is a form of ESP where a psychic touches or holds an object and receives information about the object or its owner. It is considered the parapsychology phenomenon of distance knowledge.

It has been said that those that have the ability of psychometry also have other abilities such as clairsentience and clairvoyance.

When a psychic touches an object, you can pick up any energy left behind (imprinted) on the object by its owner or those that have touched the object recently. Some have also said that it is in the never ending sharing of energy that we connect to each other.

**Exercise**
**To enhance your connection with your tools of choice.**

Take 3 deep breaths in and focus your energy on the 7 chakra points in your body one at a time until you feel them all opening up. Sit up very straight with your feet firmly on the floor and start to feel yourself relax and slow down.

• Start by focussing your energy on the base chakra – feel the red spiral opening at the base of your spine.
• Then the sacral chakra below your navel – an orange Katharine wheel.
• Focus on the solar plexus just above your navel – a yellow circle should be whizzing round getting faster and bigger.

• Go to your heart centre – see the pink and green spiral as this opens up.

• Focus all of your energy on your throat chakra – see the colour blue, thank spirit for your psychic voice.

• Focus your intention on your third eye – see the indigo spiral as your brow chakra (third eye) opens up.

• Finally and only when all of the chakras are open, focus on your crown chakra at the top of your head – see the Violet spiral opening your soul and call in your guides.

• Take 3 very deep breaths in through your nose and out through your mouth.

• Focus on an area of your past that was a huge change for you. Or an area of your past where you feel you still need guidance to understand.

• Pick up a tool of your choice – you may be holding a crystal right now, looking in the crystal ball or shuffling the angel cards – YOU MAY BE HANDS FREE – this is absolutely fine.

• Ask yourself, your soul and your guide what lesson you learnt from this and if there are more lessons to learn. Feel your tool of choice connect with you as if you were one. The connection is much more important than the answer at this stage. If you are holding your tool, feel it in your hand as if it were an extension of you.

- You may get a feeling, hear a word, see a colour, you may see a symbol – note down what you see, feel, hear or know. Ask your guides to give you more information on this if you choose to use guides.
- Thank your guide, tools and higher self for helping you with this situation.
- Close all of your chakras by switching off the imaginary light next to each chakra one by one and put a shield over your solar plexus just above the navel (very important).
- Take 3 short sharp breaths
- Wiggle your toes and fingers
- Pretend you have roots on the bottom of your feet to ground you
- Come back in to the room.

By completing this exercise you are connecting with your tools. It does not matter what the tool is supposed to do; it is your psychic connection that matters. You may find that you did not have a guide coming forward or that you did not feel anything – remember everyone is different – forget about ego and develop at your own pace. Some people never ever hear anything some people never use guides – there is no right or wrong!
I did this exercise with you, I asked why I have been single for the past five years - I held my clear quartz crystal and was told "for confidence". What did you feel?

## Homework

If you can, use an object from a friend / loved one or family member at this stage. Take a piece of jewellery from them or a watch (Psychometry).

Repeat the exercise above with their jewellery in your handNote anything you see, feel, hear and know using the correct terminology! (Clairvoyance etc) Check with your friend to see whether they resonate with your findings

MOST IMPORTANTLY REMEMBER TO SHUT DOWN AFTER THIS SECTION.

# Section 7
## Quiz

---

1. What colour is the heart chakra?

2. Where is the solar plexus chakra?

3. What is the word for a 'feeling' psychic?

4. What makes you claircognizant?

5. Name 2 crystals that could help during psychic development?

6. Why is closing down so important after each psychic session?

# Chapter 5
# Continuing Your Journey

So you've got this far, but this is just the start of your journey.

Wondering what to do with your gift?
Wondering where to go now?

When you feel ready to go further, and only when YOU feel it is time, I would like you to join me on our spiritual quest together at my School of Accredited Teachers.

The Tiffany Wardle school of spiritual teaching joins a collective of spiritual minds. We offer seminars hosted by myself or lead by our accredited teachers.

Tiffany Wardle's Certified School Seminar offers:
• A chance to have all of your questions answered about your psyshic development.

• The school will help you on your journey to a deeper level of psychic development.

• You will learn new skills from psychics such as myself.

• You will learn new channeled messages from angels and guides within the room.

• You will have a chance to feel the energy in the room from like minded people.

• You will be part of a group attunement hosted by an accredited teacher or myself.
• During the group attunement you will feel the energy of the room.

• Your senses will be heightened as we raise the frequency in the room.

• During this group attunement you will experience new spiritual heights to help you get to a deeper level of spirituality.

This and many other seminars are held globally. We also offer the "Psychic Like Me Certified Course" and other teacher training.

Please look at my website for further information on how to join Tiffany Wardle's Certified School and become an "Angel In Training".

www.angelsintraining.co.uk
www.tiffanywardle.com

Other Books by Tiffany Wardle


## The Chakra Chapter:
Chakra Colour Therapy With The Angels


## Learn Lemurian:
A journey home to the motherland


**All published via vintagewisdomltd.com**

Angels In Training

# Skinny Gal

Do you want to achieve your perfect body? Would you like to lose 7lbs in 7 days like Tiffany did?

If you want to get to your optimum size and fitness level, this programme is for you.

This truly unique and incredible work contains a series of sound and movement meditations. By listening to these meditations you can to achieve the body shape you have always dreamed of.

The author states that by listening to 4 short meditations throughout the day for just 7 days you can manifest your healthy body shape and fitness goals.

Just 30 minutes of meditation a day is all you need. This programme includes ancient wisdom, meridian tapping, sound and movement meditation all focused on showing you how to reveal your gorgeous new physique, just like Tiffany did.

**www.angelsintraining.co.uk**

84

Lightning Source UK Ltd.
Milton Keynes UK
UKOW032037120613

212175UK00014B/315/P